YESHUA
THE BUILDER
FROM BETHLEHEM TO THE BAPTISM

DAMIANO B. CENTOLA

EXPLORA BOOKS
700 – 838 West Hastings St. Vancouver, BC V6C 0A6
www.explorabooks.com
Phone: (604) 330 6795

Because of the dynamic nature of the Internet, any web addresses or links contained in this book may have changed since publication and may no longer be valid. The views expressed in this work are solely those of the author and do not necessarily reflect the views of the publisher, and the publisher hereby disclaims any responsibility for them.

Bible verses are quoted from the King James Version (KJV), which is public domain, the English Standard Version (ESV), and the New King James Version (NKJV).

ISBN: 978-1-997587-77-4 (Paperback)
978-1-83430-056-6 (Hardback)
978-1-83430-057-3 (eBook)

YESHUA
THE BUILDER
FROM BETHLEHEM TO THE BAPTISM

Table of Contents

CHAPTER ONE

Born in Bethlehem, Destined for Glory

In the silence of a Judean night, under the gaze of eternity and stars older than time, Heaven touched earth —not in thunder or fire, but in the soft breath of a newborn. Bethlehem, a town of prophecy and obscurity, became the gateway of the divine. There, under a weather-worn roof intended for beasts and burden, a child was born. Not just a child, but The Son of God, swaddled in humility, wrapped not only in cloth but in the fullness of prophetic destiny. Heaven had waited. The angels, who once beheld the breathless moment of creation, now bent low to witness something deeper: Incarnation. The Word that shaped galaxies now lay wordless in a manger. The Light that burned before the sun now flickered behind infant eyelids. The Lamb who would be slain was born among lambs raised for temple sacrifice. God had stepped into flesh—into fragility, into time, into the heartbeat of humanity.

Bethlehem: More Than a Town

Beth-lechem, "House of Bread." The name itself groans with divine intention. It was not by chance that the Bread of Life (John 6:35) would be born in a house named for sustenance.

Bethlehem was small—so small it was almost forgotten among the cities of Judah. But Micah had spoken:

> *"But you, Bethlehem Ephrathah, though you are small among the clans of Judah, out of you will come for Me one who will be ruler over Israel, whose origins are from of old, from ancient times."*
> *—Micah 5:2*

This ruler would not rise from Rome's throne or Herod's palace, but from the dust of a forgotten town. He would not wear robes woven in purple or be crowned with gold—not yet. His royalty would first be wrapped in cloths laid upon straw. He would arrive as bread for the hungry, not thunder for the powerful.

It was Caesar Augustus, the Roman emperor, who issued the decree for a census—a motion of empire meant to demonstrate control, and yet, in doing so, he unwittingly played a part in fulfilling a prophecy older than his crown. Mary and Joseph were forced to return to Bethlehem, the ancestral city of David, Joseph's lineage, to be registered. A global movement for political dominance became Heaven's escort to deliver the Messiah exactly where he was meant to be born.

In the divine economy, even emperors serve the King.

Joseph the Builder, Mary the Vessel

Joseph is often cast in shadow. But in Heaven's architecture, he is foundational. A righteous man—a just man—he bore disgrace without bitterness, obeyed visions without delay, and loved Mary with a steady hand that shaped both home and heart.

He was a tekton, often translated "carpenter," but more accurately a craftsman, builder, or stonemason—a man who shaped hard materials into strong dwellings. Joseph did not build with theories. He built with weight, with pressure, with calluses formed by years of lifting and shaping.

He taught his craft to the Son of God.

Imagine the sacred irony— Joseph showing young Yeshua how to strike stone, how to measure wood, how to find the grain and follow it. All the while, Yeshua knew the deeper grain—the grain of history, of humanity, of the human heart. He who shaped the mountains now listened to his earthly father teach him to chisel a cornerstone.

Mary, whose "yes" to God rewrote history. Her womb became the Holy of Holies. She did not carry a symbol. She carried a soul. She did not birth a metaphor. She birthed Messiah. Every contraction was prophecy pressing against time. Every breath she drew in labor was a preparation for the cries of Calvary.

She was young, but Heaven does not measure usefulness by years. Gabriel did not look for age or status; he looked for faith. "Be it unto me according to Your word," she said (Luke 1:38). And with that, the Word entered her.

The Manger and the Message

When the time came for Mary to give birth, the inns were full. The world had no room for the Maker of worlds. The irony is painful.

God's Son had to be born where animals fed because humanity's doors were already closed to Him.

Yet it was precisely in that place—a stable, a manger— that God chose to reveal Himself. It is fitting. For Yeshua came not to elevate the elite, but to descend into the dirt. The feeding trough became a throne. The stable became a cathedral.

The same hands that would one day touch lepers, lift children, and be pierced by nails now clenched around his mother's finger. The Word was learning to speak. The Light was wrapped in shadows. Divinity had made its home in dependency.

The First Witnesses: Shepherds of the Lamb

The angelic announcement was not sent to scribes, Pharisees, or kings. It was delivered to shepherds. Men of the field. Men whose days were measured in dust and silence. They were not noble by social rank, but they were noble in purpose.

These were not random laborers—they were likely tending flocks destined for the Temple sacrifices in Jerusalem. These shepherds were familiar with lambs born to die. So, when the angel appeared declaring, "Do not be afraid. I bring you good news that will cause great joy for all the people. Today in the town of David a Savior has been born to you; he is the Messiah, the Lord" (Luke 2:10–11), they understood more than most.

They ran to the manger. No delay. No hesitation. The same urgency that guarded sheep from wolves now drove them to see the Lamb of God. They knelt, and in their eyes—weathered by moonlight and miles—tears formed.

Mary's Heart: A Silent Scroll

After the shepherds left, praising God, the text says, "But Mary treasured up all these things and pondered them in her heart" (Luke 2:19). This is more than a maternal meditation. Mary was a living scroll. Her heart held Heaven's secrets.

She had seen angels. She had felt the Son of God kick from within. She had delivered the Deliverer. The shepherds have now arrived, uninvited yet foretold, declaring the glory of this moment. Mary pondered not just the events but the weight of them. She bore the burden of divine silence— knowing who her son was, yet watching him nurse, sleep, and weep like any other child.

What does it mean to raise the One who raised the world? What does it feel like to kiss the mouth that spoke stars into existence? She didn't speak. She pondered.

The Stone Beneath the Cradle

Bethlehem was built upon limestone. The ground was not soft. The homes were hewn from stone. And so was the culture—firm, shaped by tradition and toil. Yeshua's first surroundings were not abstract or philosophical—they were tangible, weighty, enduring. This is no accident. Stone would become a recurring theme in his ministry:

> *He would call himself the cornerstone (Matthew 21:42).*
> *He would say, "Upon this rock I will build my church"*
> *—(Matthew 16:18).*

> *The stone the builders rejected would become the capstone*
> *—Psalm 118:22*

The Law was given on tablets of stone; now Grace had come in the flesh.

Yeshua was born into a world of stone, but his mission was to turn stony hearts into hearts of flesh (Ezekiel 36:26). He would not just build homes—he would build people. And the first stones were laid in Bethlehem.

The Hidden Weight of Joseph

Joseph remained silent in Scripture. We have no recorded words from him.

Yet his silence is not emptiness—it is strength. He listened to dreams, obeyed Heaven's commands, and built a safe world for the Son of God.

He bore the shame of a pregnancy he did not initiate. He bore the burden of traveling with a pregnant woman. He bore the task of fleeing to Egypt. And yet he did not speak a word of complaint.

In Joseph we see a father not by flesh, but by faith. His trade shaped his hands. His obedience shaped Yeshua's early world.

Imagine the long days at the quarry. The sweat. The hammers. The rhythm of stone against stone. And then coming home to cradle the infant Messiah, kiss Mary's forehead, and dream again of angelic warnings.

Yeshua's humanity was not formed in luxury but in labor. Not in temples but in tool sheds. Not among scribes but under the teaching of a man who shaped stone with reverence and hands that trembled at God's word.

Conclusion: Foundations Set in Straw and Stone

The story of Bethlehem is not just the story of a birth—it is the laying of a foundation.

It is the first stone in the construction of the Kingdom of God.

It is the moment when Heaven stooped low enough to enter a woman's womb, be born beside animals, and be held by hands rough with labor.

The manger held not only a baby—it held prophecy, divinity, and the hope of nations.

And though kings slept unaware, and the elite remained uninformed, the heavens opened wide to announce:

The Builder has come.

He will build not with nails alone, but with mercy.

He will cut not only wood, but through human pride.

He will raise not only beams, but the dead.

He will shape not only doorposts, but disciples.

He will build not just homes — but a Kingdom that will never pass away. Born in Bethlehem. Destined for Glory.

Historical Clarification: The Visit of the Magi

Before we leave Bethlehem and journey with Joseph, Mary, and Yeshua into exile, it's important to pause and correct a popular misunderstanding. The arrival of the wise men—the magi—did not happen the night Yeshua was born.

Contrary to many nativity scenes, the magi were not at the manger. The Gospel of Matthew tells us that the magi visited Yeshua in a house (Matthew 2:11), not a stable, and they saw a child (Greek: paidion), not a newborn (brephos). Based on Herod's paranoid decree to kill all boys two years old and under (Matthew 2:16), it is likely that Yeshua was somewhere between 12 to 24 months old when the magi arrived.

They had followed the star for many months—possibly up to two years—traveling from the East, perhaps from Persia or Babylon, studying prophecies and signs. Their arrival was not part of the birth night, but a separate

event, one that occurred long enough after the birth for the family to settle into a house in Bethlehem.

This matters. It reminds us that the story of Yeshua's coming was not a one-night wonder. It unfolded over time—through journeys, dreams, delays, dangers, and divine protection. The magi's gifts—gold, frankincense, and myrrh— were not delivered to a newborn king on straw, but to a toddler king in a modest dwelling, watched over by two humble parents who had learned to trust the voice of God more than the chaos of men.

So, as we move now into the next chapter—into danger, into Egypt, into exile—know this: God was already protecting Yeshua long after the manger, through every step of his childhood. The magi came not to confirm a myth, but to worship a living.

King already beginning to grow in wisdom and stature.

CHAPTER TWO

The Refugee Messiah: Egypt and Exile

The star had faded, and the silence had returned. The magi had come and gone, kneeling not before a newborn in a manger but before a child in a modest house. Their gifts—gold, frankincense, and myrrh—glinted with prophetic weight. They left by another road, warned in a dream to avoid Herod, that murderous shadow cast over a restless kingdom.

And that same night, another dream came—not to scholars or kings, but to a builder.

Joseph, whose quiet obedience had already rewritten history once, was roused by the voice of an angel.

> *"Get up. Take the child and his mother and escape to Egypt. Stay there until I tell you, for Herod is going to search for the child to kill him"*
> *—Matthew 2:13*

The command was not softened with explanation. There was no comfort, no delay, no room for hesitation. Danger was imminent. Death was near. The same Herod who feigned interest in worshiping the Messiah was already plotting the massacre of innocent children—an attempt to erase prophecy with blood.

Joseph did not argue. He did not wait until dawn. He did what fathers do when the life of a child is at stake: he rose and went. In the middle of the night, he took Mary and the young Yeshua and fled south, into uncertainty, into exile, into Egypt.

Into the Land of Egypt

Egypt. The land of Pharaohs and prophets. The place of slavery and salvation. It had once received Jacob's family during famine and later enslaved their descendants for four hundred years.

Egypt was both a womb and a grave for Israel. And now, for the second time in history, a Hebrew child destined to deliver his people would find safety in its borders.

"Out of Egypt I called My son."
—Hosea 11:1

Matthew would later quote this verse, not as a simple historical observation, but as a divine pattern repeating itself. Just as Moses had been drawn out of Egypt to lead the Israelites to freedom, so too would Yeshua emerge from Egypt— not to deliver his people from Pharaoh, but from sin, death, and despair.

In this moment, Yeshua became a refugee. Not metaphorically. Not symbolically. But literally. The Son of God, born under the stars of Bethlehem, now walked as a displaced child, hidden in a foreign land, dependent on the hospitality of strangers and the protection of divine providence.

It's here—between borders and barrenness—that Yeshua's humanity deepened. He did not come to the safe and settled. He came as one who would know the sting of displacement, the language of longing, the ache of not belonging. His feet, even as a child, touched the dust of exile.

The Cost of Obedience

We must not romanticize this journey. Joseph and Mary were not escorted by guards. They were not provided safe passage or gold-paved roads. They were poor. They had no political clout. Their only provision came from Heaven—and the costly gifts the magi had delivered, which likely financed their survival.

Imagine the weight on Joseph's shoulders. Not only was he tasked with providing for a wife and child—he was now the guardian of God's Messiah, forced to uproot and navigate through desert roads, unpredictable caravans, and a foreign culture. He was not a preacher. He was not a prophet. He was a tekton—a builder—now called to build safety in a foreign land.

And Mary, still a teenager, now bore the burden of motherhood under threat.

Her lullabies were sung in whispers. Her prayers were soaked in vigilance. She was raising the Deliverer while being delivered herself. The cost of obedience was high. But both Joseph and Mary knew this journey was not theirs to control—it was God's to command.

The Massacre of the Innocents

While the holy family settled quietly into Egypt, a massacre bled through the streets of Bethlehem.

Herod's fury, fueled by insecurity and satanic fear, erupted into genocide. Every boy under two years old was slaughtered—a desperate attempt to destroy a king he could not name. It was not the first time a ruler had targeted Hebrew boys.

Pharaoh had done it in Moses' day. But now, Herod followed the same ancient pattern of fear-driven slaughter.

The Gospel of Matthew records:

> *"A voice is heard in Ramah, weeping and great*
> *mourning, Rachel weeping for her children and*
> *refusing to be comforted, because they are no more."*
> *—Matthew 2:18*

Rachel, the matriarch of Israel, becomes the symbol of collective grief— mourning not only for her own descendants but for the countless nameless ones lost in the wake of political evil.

The Bible does not say Yeshua was spared because he was special. He was spared because Joseph listened. Because Mary obeyed. Because God intervened.

This matters. Because it shows us something sacred: Yeshua's safety was not insulated by divine force fields or angelic armies standing visible on every corner. He was protected through faith, dreams, obedience, and timely movement. God worked through the human fabric of trust, warning, and action.

Egypt: A Place of Waiting and Becoming

The Scriptures do not record what life in Egypt looked like. We don't know how long they stayed—perhaps two or three years. We don't know where exactly they lived or how they survived each day. But we do know God was there.

Egypt, once a symbol of bondage, became a place of refuge. And in that paradox lies the poetry of the Gospel. Yeshua was hidden in the very place that had once oppressed his ancestors. He was protected in the house of former captors.

It's likely that Joseph continued his trade, building with stone and wood, carving out both a living and a sanctuary for his family. And Mary would have continued nurturing, teaching, and praying— knowing that every breath her son took was a breath toward destiny.

In Egypt, the holy family waited. They were not idle. They were growing. Yeshua, still a child, was learning what it meant to dwell among strangers. He was absorbing language, watching trade, seeing how nations lived beyond the borders of Israel. And perhaps, even then, he began to understand the global scope of his mission—not just to Israel, but to all nations.

A Return Called by Heaven

Eventually, the call came. Another dream. Another message.

> *"Those who were trying to take the child's life are dead." —Matthew 2:20*

Herod had died. The one who had tried to snuff out the Light of the world had fallen into darkness himself. The danger had passed. Joseph once again obeyed. He took Mary and Yeshua and began the journey home. But as they neared Judea, Joseph learned that Herod's son, Archelaus, ruled in his father's place— a cruel and unstable successor. Once again, God spoke through a dream, redirecting them north to Galilee, to a town small and overlooked. To Nazareth:

> *"So was fulfilled what was said through the prophets, that he would be called a Nazarene."*
> *—Matthew 2:23*

Nazareth was not prestigious. It was a town of mixed reputation, even mockery. "Can anything good come from Nazareth?" Nathanael would later ask (John 1:46). But for Yeshua, it was home. It was sanctuary. It was soil for growth.

The Refugee King and the Kingdom to Come

Let us pause and absorb the reality of what we've witnessed:

Yeshua was a refugee. Yeshua was hunted.

Yeshua lived in exile. Yeshua returned not in triumph but in silence.

Before the ministry came the movement. Before the baptism came
the barrenness. Before the miracles came the misplacement.

He who would one day say, "Foxes have dens and birds have nests,
but the Son of Man has no place to lay his head" (Matthew 8:20),
had already lived that truth long before he spoke it.

Yeshua did not begin his life in comfort. He began in crisis.

He did not grow up with privilege. He grew up with pressure.

He was not guarded by systems. He was guarded by Heaven.

And it is here that we begin to understand the kind of Savior he
would become—not detached, not untouchable, but deeply
identified with the world's most vulnerable.

The immigrant. The forgotten.

The laborer. The threatened. The obedient.

The watched. The preserved.

He was all of them—and more.

The Carpenter in Exile

And Joseph—oh, Joseph. Still no words from him in the text. But
again, we hear him through his actions.

He carried the Word of God across borders.

He built protection with hands meant for stone.

He raised the Son of God in a foreign land without complaint.

Joseph is a prototype of spiritual fatherhood— strong, obedient,
responsive, and invisible. The world did not honor him. History
seldom speaks of him. But the Kingdom was built upon the quiet
scaffolding of his faith.

Conclusion: The Exodus Begins Again

Yeshua's first years were a reenactment of Israel's history. Born under prophetic stars. Sent into Egypt. Brought out by divine call. Led through danger.

Settled in Nazareth.

The true Exodus was beginning again. But this time, the Deliverer was not outside the people. He was one of them. One with them. He had walked in their sandals. He had felt their fears.

The Messiah had not come only to save.

He had come to walk, to wait, to wander, and to become.

And as he took his first steps back on the soil of Galilee, the world had no idea that the Kingdom had already come—hidden in a refugee child, sleeping safely in Nazareth, cradled by a carpenter, watched over by Heaven.

CHAPTER THREE

Nazareth: A Builder's School of Obedience

Nazareth.

The very word drips with obscurity. In Yeshua's time, it was not known for beauty, wealth, or prestige. It was no city of kings, no center of study, no place of pilgrimage. It lay nestled in the Galilean hills—dusty, rocky, removed from the political and spiritual centers of the nation. To many, it was a forgotten village.

Yet it was here, in this place dismissed by men, that the Son of God would grow into manhood.

> *"He shall be called a Nazarene."*
> *—Matthew 2:23*

There was no single Old Testament prophecy that used those exact words, but the phrase echoes a collective whisper from the prophets: that the Messiah would be despised, overlooked, and lowly. In Nazareth, Yeshua's identity as a humble servant was not just foretold—it was formed.

The Return Home

After Egypt, the journey northward into Galilee was likely long and cautious.

Archelaus, Herod's son, was still in power in Judea, and Joseph knew the threat had not vanished—it had simply shifted. That's why the family settled in Nazareth, far from the center of political power, tucked away among the working poor.

It wasn't home in the traditional sense. Bethlehem was the ancestral city of David. Egypt had become a temporary refuge. But Nazareth would become the soil where Yeshua would be planted. It was where he would run, fall, learn, listen, and grow. It was where he would be known—not as Rabbi, Messiah, or King—but as "the carpenter's son."

There is something profound in that simplicity. The Creator of all things would choose to be known only by his earthly father's reputation for thirty years.

The Word would be silent. The Light would wait. The Messiah would remain hidden.

The Workshop and the World

Joseph's hands, seasoned by years of craftsmanship, now shaped the life of the one through whom all things were made. The tools of his trade—hammer, chisel, level, rope, plumb line— were the same tools Yeshua would come to master.

Though often translated "carpenter," the Greek word tekton means much more. It describes a builder, a craftsman—likely someone who worked more with stone than with wood, given the terrain of Galilee.

Nazareth's hills offered stone, not cedar. And so Yeshua learned to build with that which was heavy, resistant, enduring.

We imagine the workshop— sunlight angling in through rough beams, the scent of limestone dust and olive wood in the air. The rhythmic echo of hammer to stone, day after day.

Yeshua's young hands blistering, callousing, strengthening. His arms shaping beams and grinding edges.

He did not begin as a preacher. He began as a laborer.

He did not first lift scrolls. He lifted stones.

He did not come with titles. He came with tenacity.

Every moment in that workshop was preparation.

Not wasted. Not mundane. Sacred.

For in shaping walls, he learned how to shape words. In measuring foundations, he learned how to reveal truths.

In carrying beams, he anticipated the weight of a cross.

Obedience: The Silent Curriculum

The Scriptures say little about Yeshua's youth. Just one verse gives us the entire curriculum of his early years:

> *"And Jesus grew in wisdom and stature, and in favor*
> *with God and man."*
> *—Luke 2:52*

This is not a throwaway sentence. It is an entire theology of formation.

He grew, not just physically, but mentally, spiritually, and relationally.

He was not born fully formed in understanding. He grew in wisdom.

He had to learn language. He had to observe relationships. He had to understand Torah not only as God but as student.

Though divine, he submitted himself to the process of learning, honoring the structures of family, community, and faith.

The Son of God became a son of man, and he did not skip steps.

This is a rebuke to the impatient. To those who want to bypass the process and jump to the platform.

Yeshua waited. For thirty years, he waited. Thirty years of chopping, lifting, shaping, and silence.

Not one sermon. Not one miracle.

Not one crowd. Just obedience.

And this—this silent obedience—was not lesser. It was foundational. It was the school of obedience, and it happened in a place no one expected, doing work most would overlook.

Mary's Gaze, Joseph's Silence

Imagine Mary watching her son in the shop, his arms growing strong, his eyes serious with focus. Every time he smoothed a stone or wiped sweat from his brow, she must have remembered Gabriel's words:

> *"He will be great and will be called the Son of the Most High."*
> *—Luke 1:32*

And yet... he was just building chairs. Just shaping doorways. Just repairing roofs.

Wasn't he supposed to be doing more? Wasn't he supposed to rule? But Mary had learned not to rush God. She had pondered too many things already. She understood that what looks like delay is often divine strategy. She kept watching, kept trusting, kept loving.

And Joseph? We still hear no words. But his presence echoes louder than a sermon. He remained. He taught. He worked. He led. And then—at some point unknown to us—he died.

We are left to imagine Yeshua standing at his earthly father's grave, grief carving new lines into his young face, understanding loss before he ever healed the grieving. This man who had taught him so much— who had protected him, instructed him, loved him— was gone.

In that moment, Yeshua learned something no book could teach: sorrow.

He would one day be called a man of sorrows (Isaiah 53:3), and perhaps that title began not with the suffering of Gethsemane but with the death of Joseph.

Shaped in Nazareth, Rejected by Nazareth

Nazareth did not become proud of its Messiah. It became blind to him.

Years later, when Yeshua returned to preach in the synagogue, the people were astonished—not because they saw him as divine, but because they couldn't accept that someone so familiar could be so anointed.

> *"Is this not the carpenter, the son of Mary...?"*
> *—Mark 6:3*

"And they took offense at him."

Nazareth trained him. But Nazareth also rejected him.

It is a tragic truth that the places that form us can sometimes refuse to receive us. Yeshua was not surprised. He would later say, "A prophet is not without honor except in his own town, among his relatives and in his own home." (Mark 6:4)

But this rejection was not a failure. It was part of the formation. Nazareth had done its job. It had shaped the Savior with stone, silence, obscurity, and resistance. It had taught him how to be misunderstood.

And it had prepared him to endure it again—and again—for the sake of the world.

The Hidden Messiah Among the Laborers

For decades, Yeshua lived among people who had no idea who he truly was. He was simply known as the builder's son, the stone shaper, the quiet neighbor, the one who always helped when someone's wall caved in or beam split.

But what they didn't know was that the one building homes among them was also building a Kingdom.

What they didn't see was that the one repairing broken foundations would one day be the foundation. The one smoothing stone would one day roll away a stone to conquer death.

This is our Messiah. Not distant.

Not decorated. Not detached.

But deeply embedded in the dust, sweat, and weight of life.

Conclusion: The Preparation of a King

Nazareth was the place of becoming. The hidden years were not a waste—they were the workshop of Heaven.

There, in obscurity:

Yeshua grew in wisdom.

He learned the trade of his earthly father.

He experienced loss.

He endured rejection.

He waited in obedience.

He was being fitted—stone by stone—for the temple he would one day raise.

Before he called disciples, he obeyed his parents.

Before he opened the Scriptures in synagogues, he opened his hands to work.

Before he stood on a mountain to teach, he stood in a shop to build.

This is the Messiah we follow.

Not just the Savior on the cross,

But the builder in Nazareth. The obedient Son.

The quiet King.

The cornerstone in disguise.

CHAPTER FOUR

Tekton: The Hands That Shaped Stone

He shaped stone before he shaped souls.

Before the world ever heard his voice on a mountain or saw him stretch out his hands to heal, Yeshua's hands were already at work—firm, patient, and deliberate. Long before he opened blind eyes, those same fingers gripped the raw edge of limestone.

Before he called fishermen to follow him, he learned to read the grain of olive wood and strike it with just the right force.

He was a tekton—a builder, a craftsman. The Greek word does not limit him to carpentry as we often picture it. Tekton referred to anyone skilled in construction—especially in stonework, which was far more common than woodworking in the rocky terrain of Galilee.

This was no accident. The God who formed Adam from dust now formed tables, walls, and beams with his hands. The One who shaped the mountains of Sinai now shaped stones in Nazareth.

And in that sacred silence of labor, something eternal was being prepared.

The Geography of Stone

To understand Yeshua as a tekton, we must understand his land. Northern Israel is not rich in forests—it is a region of rock. Homes, foundations, synagogues, and even water cisterns were carved into or built from stone. Wood was precious, but stone was everywhere. Yeshua likely worked in nearby Sepphoris, a Romanized city under construction just four miles from Nazareth. Herod Antipas had declared it the jewel of Galilee, and its rebuilding would have required skilled artisans.

Builders from the surrounding regions, including Joseph and Yeshua, were likely hired for its stone roads, villas, and arches. Imagine the adolescent Messiah walking to Sepphoris with tools strapped across his back. The Son of God rising before the sun, walking dirt paths to labor among Roman officials and Hebrew workers alike—blisters on his hands, sweat on his brow, dust on his tunic.

This is the Jesus we forget— the builder among builders, the tekton among men, the Creator of the world stooping to carve it piece by piece.

The Theology of Labor

In Eden, man was given the task to tend and keep the garden (Genesis 2:15). Work was not a punishment—it was a purpose. Labor was holy long before it became exhausting. And in Yeshua, we see the restoration of that sacred rhythm.

His time as a tekton was not incidental. It was formative. He wasn't biding time until ministry began—he was living the ministry of patience, precision, humility, and strength. He was learning to endure. To carry weight. To remain faithful in the unseen.

Every stone he carried, he carried with purpose.

Every beam he cut, he cut with care.

Every foundation he laid, he laid with the wisdom of one who knew the weight of eternal things.

And this was not just about craft—it was about calling. Yeshua's understanding of humanity's burdens wasn't theoretical. It was experiential. He bore the heat, the pressure, the delay, the repetition, the injustice of underpaid labor, the ache in his back after a long day of hauling material for someone else's house.

The builder who would one day declare, "Come to me, all who are weary and burdened, and I will give you rest" (Matthew 11:28), knew exactly what it meant to be weary and burdened.

The Calloused Hands of God

We often imagine God with outstretched, clean hands, lifted in power or blessing. But Yeshua's hands were calloused. He had splinters, cuts, and dust ground into his palms. His fingerprints were pressed into clay and stone. He didn't just bless the earth—he worked it.

Imagine this: The same hands that molded galaxies in the beginning were now gripping hammers and chisels. The same fingers that would one day touch the blind and lift the dead were now smoothing the edge of a table. The same arms that would stretch across a cross were now steadying a beam on a rooftop.

This is the paradox of the Incarnation.

The Maker became the mender.

The Architect became the apprentice.

The Word became a worker.

Yeshua didn't float into ministry. He built his way toward it. With sweat, silence, and sacred effort.

The Language of a Builder

When Yeshua finally emerged into public ministry, his language revealed the labor of his life.

> *"Everyone who hears these words of mine and puts them into practice is like a wise man who built his house on the rock."*
> *—Matthew 7:24*

> *"No one can serve two masters... You cannot serve both God and Mammon."*
> *—Matthew 6:24*
> *"Which of you, if he wants to build a tower, does not first sit down and count the cost?"*
> *—Luke 14:28*

These are not abstract metaphors. These are the words of a builder. One who knew the value of laying foundations. One who understood the danger of haste and the cost of construction. His teachings carry the weight of lived experience.

Even his ministry reflected a builder's mindset:

Blueprint – His parables laid the framework of the Kingdom.

Foundation – He chose disciples and began to shape them one by one.

Cornerstone – He placed himself at the center of a new spiritual structure.

Materials – He used the weak, the rejected, the broken to build something holy.

Completion – His final words on the cross? "It is finished." The work was done.

The Stones the Builders Rejected Yeshua's path would mirror the very materials he worked with—stone.

> *"The stone the builders rejected has become the*
> *cornerstone."*
> *—Psalm 118:22*

He knew what it was to select stones—examining each one for flaws, weight, shape, and strength. Not every stone was suitable. Some were discarded. Some were passed over. Some seemed unfit for use.

But God chose what men rejected.

Yeshua became that stone— rejected by the religious builders of his day, dismissed by the elite, overlooked by the powerful. And yet, he was the one the Father would place as the chief cornerstone of a new temple—not built with hands, but with hearts.

Even Peter, his disciple and a fellow laborer, would later write:

> *"You also, like living stones, are being built into a*
> *spiritual house..."*
> *—1 Peter 2:5*

Because once you've been shaped by the Builder, you become a builder yourself.

The Cross: The Final Beam

The final object Yeshua would lift and carry was not a beam in a home or a column in a courtyard—it was a cross. A heavy piece of timber, rough and splintered, laid upon his shoulders.

He knew how to carry beams.

He had done it all his life.

But this one—this final beam—was different. It was not for a roof. It was for redemption.

The same shoulders that bore stones and wood now bore the sins of the world. The same hands that had carved and shaped now stretched wide to be nailed. The same calloused palms that built homes now bled to build a new covenant.

The Builder became the Sacrifice.

The Architect became the Offering.

The Craftsman became the Cornerstone of Salvation.

Conclusion: Built to Endure

Yeshua's years as a tekton were not a footnote—they were a foundation. His craftsmanship was not incidental—it was intentional. It shaped his metaphors, his ministry, and his mission.

He was never just a carpenter.

He was the Builder of all things.

Builder of homes. Builder of people. Builder of a Kingdom. Builder of eternity.

And now, even still, he builds.

> *"I go to prepare a place for you..."*
> *—John 14:2*

The Builder hasn't stopped building.

He is preparing foundations in hearts.

He is chiseling away what is weak in us.

He is aligning our lives to match his divine design.

He is shaping the Church, stone by stone, into something that will endure forever.

He is building something in you.

And he knows exactly what he's doing.

CHAPTER FIVE

The Boy in the Temple: Twelve and Timeless

It was the first time he stayed behind.

The sun had already begun to descend behind Jerusalem's hills when Mary noticed. The crowd around her was dense—friends, cousins, familiar faces from Galilee all walking the well- worn road home after Passover. But one face was missing.

Yeshua.

He was twelve. Not a toddler to be held. Not a child to be constantly watched. He was of age now—able to walk among the men, to listen with the elders. And so, like many families on pilgrimage, they had assumed he was among the company.

Until he wasn't. Panic rose like heat.

Joseph's steps quickened. Mary's heart pounded. They turned back toward Jerusalem, retracing every step. Every alley, every square, every doorway. The city was still full, echoing with the remnants of the festival. But their son— God's Son—was gone.

The Journey to Jerusalem

Every year, Yeshua's family made the journey from Nazareth to Jerusalem for the Feast of Passover, as prescribed in the Torah (Exodus 12; Deuteronomy 16:1–8). The trip, nearly ninety miles one way, was more than obligation—it was devotion.

For Joseph and Mary, it meant leaving behind work, enduring the rigors of travel, carrying food and supplies for days, and sleeping in crowded quarters. For Yeshua, it meant walking among songs, seeing the hills of Judea, feeling the swell of anticipation as the holy city came into view.

But this time was different. Yeshua was twelve. He had entered the stage of Jewish boyhood when a young man begins to take on the yoke of the Law. Though the bar mitzvah ceremony as we know it came later, Jewish boys at twelve were already expected to study, recite, and walk in the commandments.

Yeshua was now standing on the threshold between childhood and manhood— not only biologically, but spiritually. And he was not walking through that door lightly.

Found in the Temple Three days passed.

Three days.

It is not lost on the reader that the only childhood story we have of Yeshua ends with him being found—alive—in Jerusalem on the third day.

A foreshadowing, quiet and brilliant, hidden in plain sight.

> *"After three days they found him in the temple courts,*
> *sitting among the teachers, listening to them and*
> *asking them questions. Everyone who heard him was*
> *amazed at his understanding and his answers."*
> *—Luke 2:46–47*

He was not playing in the streets. He was not lost in the marketplace. He was sitting among the elders of Israel, not simply learning— but engaging. Asking questions, yes—but also answering them. And they were amazed.

At twelve, Yeshua was already teaching the teachers.

At twelve, he was already beginning to reveal the weight of who he was.

His posture was humble—he listened. But his insight was divine— he astounded.

Imagine the scene: the rabbis, wrapped in their robes, aged and lettered, leaning in toward this boy whose voice had not yet deepened, whose beard had not yet grown, and yet whose words cut like prophecy and clarity entwined.

Who is this child? they must have asked.

But even then, Yeshua wasn't seeking to impress. He was seeking to reveal.

Mary's Question, Yeshua's Answer

When Mary and Joseph finally found him, relief gave way to rebuke.

> *"Son, why have you treated us like this? Your father*
> *and I have been anxiously searching for you."*
> *—Luke 2:48*

It is the cry of every parent who has ever lost track of a child—the trembling between love and fear.

Yeshua's response was not flippant. It was full of purpose.

> *"Why were you searching for me?" he asked. "Didn't*
> *you know I had to be in my Father's house?"*
> *—Luke 2:49*

It was his first recorded words in Scripture. And like the first words of creation—"Let there be light"—they carried profound revelation.

I must be in my Father's house.

Not Joseph's house. Not the carpenter's shop. Not the roads of Nazareth.

But the Temple—the meeting place between Heaven and Earth.

Already, at twelve, Yeshua understood something deep: his identity as Son was rooted in divine presence, not simply earthly lineage.

He was not abandoning Joseph. He was clarifying mission.

He was not disobedient—he was devoted.

He was not rebelling—he was revealing.

He wasn't wandering—he was anchoring himself in his Father's house.

A Moment of Unveiling

Luke tells us plainly:

> *"But they did not understand what he was saying to them."*
> *—Luke 2:50*

How could they? The mystery was still unfolding. The child they had cradled, nursed, raised—now speaking as one who knew God, not just worshiped Him. The veil between Heaven and Earth was already thinning, and they were standing at the edge of it.

But Yeshua did not press further. He did not explain. He returned with them to Nazareth, and Luke says,

> *"He was obedient to them."*
> *—Luke 2:51*

He who had just claimed the Temple as his home submitted himself once again to obscurity.

He who amazed the scholars now returned to sanding beams and carrying stone.

He who could have stayed in the courts of teaching returned to the fields of labor.

Because it was not yet time. Wisdom and Favor.

Then the curtain closes for eighteen years. But not without this final summary:

> *"And Jesus grew in wisdom and stature, and in favor*
> *with God and man."*
> *—Luke 2:52*

This is more than a transitional verse. It is a description of formation.

Wisdom – The internal growth of mind and spirit.

Stature – The physical and personal maturity.

Favor with God – The affirmation of Heaven.

Favor with man – The integrity that drew the respect of people.

It was not instant. It was not magic.

It was growth.

Yeshua did not descend from the clouds with scrolls in his hands.

He grew. He learned. He waited.

He built. He obeyed.

He was divine—but he honored the process of human maturity.

Timeless at Twelve

At twelve, Yeshua gave the world a glimpse of eternity.

Twelve is a number of governments in Scripture:

Twelve tribes of Israel.

Twelve stones in the high priest's breastplate.

Twelve disciples who would one day be chosen by this very boy.

At twelve, he stood at the center of Israel's spiritual government—the Temple. At twelve, he revealed that the government would rest on his shoulders (Isaiah 9:6).

At twelve, the Messiah stepped out from silence and whispered eternity into time.

But then he waited eighteen more years.

The Obedient Return to Nazareth

Perhaps this is the greatest lesson of this story—not just that Yeshua was wise beyond his years, but that he was willing to wait.

He returned to Nazareth. To noise and neighbors.

To calluses and patience. To labor and laughter.

To years of seeming smallness.

The Temple would wait. The disciples would wait. The miracles would wait. The crowds, the cross, the crown—they would all wait. Because he knew the Father's voice did not rush. The one who spoke worlds into being now moved one day at a time.

This is what makes him trustworthy.

Not just that he is all- powerful, but that he is all- patient.

He understands process. He honors preparation.

He knows the value of silence, the ache of delay, and the beauty of growing into your calling.

Conclusion: When the Curtain Opens Again

The next time we see him, the Jordan will be flowing, the crowds will be gathering, and John the Baptizer will be pointing.

> *"Behold, the Lamb of God who takes away the sin of*
> *the world!"*
> *—John 1:29*

But for now, the curtain closes again.

The boy from Nazareth returns to the workshop.

The teacher of teachers lays aside his questions.

The Son of God walks home with his parents, his sandals dusty, his future quietly unfolding.

And the world turns, unaware that the one who will save it is already living among them, shaping stone, honoring his father, listening to his mother, growing in grace.

Twelve years old.

Timeless in purpose. Patient in process.

Already the King—and yet still the son.

CHAPTER SIX

The Hidden Years: The Silent Formation

The Gospels give us no further scenes, no direct quotes, no recorded miracles or teachings between the ages of twelve and thirty. Eighteen years vanish from the written record like morning mist— no flash, no noise, no fame.

But silence is not absence. And obscurity is not idleness. In the Kingdom of God, what is hidden is often what is most holy.

These years—commonly passed over, quietly tucked between the temple and the Jordan—were not empty.

They were sacred. They were formational. They were the foundation upon which eternity would stand.

God's Pattern of Hiddenness

Scripture is filled with people who were hidden before they were revealed:

- Moses spent forty years in the wilderness before leading Israel.
- David tended sheep in the fields long before he held the throne.
- Joseph endured years of slavery and prison before stepping into Pharaoh's court.
- Paul went into Arabia for three years before beginning is apostolic ministry.

God forms his greatest servants in silence.

In wildernesses.

In work.

In waiting.

The hidden years of Yeshua are no different. Though unrecorded in detail, they are not unimportant. They were the forge of his humanity, the school of patience, the altar of daily surrender.

The Long Obedience of an Ordinary Life

Imagine the rhythm. Day after day. Year after year.

Sunlight rising over Galilee.

Tools placed in hand. Stone laid upon stone. Meals shared with family. Prayers whispered at dusk. Neighbors needing repairs.

Children playing in the street.

No applause. No crowd.

No miracle.

Just work.

Just obedience. Just presence.

He who would command storms to be still spent years listening to the quiet wind on Nazareth's hills.

He who would heal lepers with a word spent years healing broken walls and bent thresholds.

He who would call the weary to rest lived the fatigue of sweat and splinters.

He was not pretending. He was becoming.

Mary's Reminders, Joseph's Absence

We are not told when Joseph died, but by the time Yeshua begins his public ministry, Joseph is never mentioned again. Tradition holds that he passed during these hidden years.

This would have left Yeshua as the eldest male in the household, responsible for his mother and younger siblings. The pressure of provision would have pressed against the call of purpose. The Son of God bore the full weight of human family duty.

Mary—his mother, his first believer, his first disciple— would have kept reminding him, not in pushy haste but in patient remembrance. She had not forgotten what the angel said. She had not lost the wonder of his birth. But she, too, submitted to the hiddenness.

She watched as her son grew into a man, as his shoulders filled out, as his beard came in, as his voice settled into strength. She pondered still. Waited still. And likely whispered to him now and again, "When the time comes…"

But the time had not yet come.

And so he waited. The Integrity of Work.

We so often underestimate the holiness of labor.

Yet these years show us that honest work, done with excellence and integrity, was the very path the Son of God chose.

There were no shortcuts. There were no signs hanging outside the shop reading "Messiah, Coming Soon." He charged fair prices. He carried what others could not lift.

He kept appointments. He built homes he would never live in. And in every beam, every doorway, every roof… he left fingerprints of perfection.

Because excellence in obscurity is a form of worship.

When no one is watching— how you work, how you treat people, how you respond to pressure—this is where Kingdom character is carved.

Yeshua didn't preach sermons on excellence.

He lived them in Nazareth, in silence, in sweat.

The Silence of the Scriptures

The Gospel writers, under divine inspiration, chose not to fill these years with speculation or stories. Why? Because what God leaves unspoken, he often intends to be witnessed through the fruit rather than the record.

These years formed in Yeshua:

Deep empathy for the human condition

Understanding of poverty and provision

Compassion for widows, workers, and wanderers

Wisdom forged in patience

Discipline built by routine

A love for the Law, not out of obligation, but delight

He grew—not only into his identity as the Messiah but into perfect obedience as the Son.

> *"Although he was a Son, he learned obedience through*
> *what he suffered."*
> *—Hebrews 5:8*

What did he suffer? Not just the Cross.

He suffered delay.

He suffered rejection. He suffered being misunderstood.

He suffered the tension of knowing who he was—and waiting until the Father said, "Now."

The Carpenter and the Calling

There is something deeply incarnational about the fact that Yeshua built with his hands.

He didn't just teach metaphors of building—he lived them:

Measuring things that had to last

Squaring what would be stood upon

Aligning beams that would hold roofs in storms

Fitting stones that had to carry weight

All of these things would echo in his ministry.

He would say:

"A house divided cannot stand."

"Build on the rock, not the sand."

"Count the cost before you build."

Why? Because he had lived it.

Because he had built it.

He knew what it took to construct something that would not crumble.

And when the time would come, he would build again—not with stone, but with people.

Not with wood, but with faith.

Not with beams, but with the Cross.

Why the Waiting?

Why not begin earlier? Why not heal at twenty? Teach at twenty-five?

Because Yeshua was not just saving us from sin.

He was stepping into the full depth of humanity.

He came not to skip ahead but to fulfill every inch of our human condition—from baby cries to adolescent wonder to adult responsibility.

He waited because waiting is part of redemption.

Every time we wonder if God has forgotten us in the shadows, we must remember:

> Yeshua lived there too. And the Kingdom was not delayed by the silence.

> It was being formed in the silence.

The Day Before the River

We are now drawing near. The final years in Nazareth have passed.

The workshop is nearly still. The tools rest. The sawdust settles.

A final sunrise in Galilee. A kiss on Mary's cheek. A quiet blessing spoken in Aramaic. And the sandals are tied one more time.

He leaves the house he built. He walks away from the town that shaped him.

He heads toward the river.

Not to begin—But to reveal what had already been begun in silence.

Conclusion: What Is Formed in You in the Silence?

Yeshua's hidden years are not merely background.

They are a mirror.

They remind us that:

> Preparation is not punishment.

> Silence is not absence.

> Obscurity is not failure.

> Work is worship.

The sacred is often quiet.

You may feel forgotten. But so did the carpenter of Nazareth.

You may feel delayed.

But so was the Son of God, and if the Father entrusted.

His only begotten Son to hidden years, then maybe you can trust

Him with yours.

CHAPTER SEVEN

Before the Baptism: The Cornerstone Is Set

The sun was rising over the Jordan Valley. The river glistened like a ribbon of promise cutting through the wilderness. The wild prophet stood waist-deep in its waters, his voice booming across the plains like thunder rolling through parched bones. "Repent, for the Kingdom of Heaven is at hand!"

And somewhere along that dusty path, among the gathering crowds of tax collectors, soldiers, and sinners, walked a man whose face was unknown but whose presence turned eternity.

He was no longer a child. He was no longer just a builder.

He was no longer just Mary's son.

He was the cornerstone— quietly, finally, fully set.

The years of silence had ended. The waiting was over. The hands that had shaped stone were now ready to shape destinies. The One who had waited in obedience for thirty years was now walking toward the waters of declaration.

The Final Morning in Nazareth

We can only imagine the morning he left.

The tools were likely still in their place—the hammer, the mallet, the chisel, the smoothing stone. The scent of cedar and olivewood hung in the air. Mary may have prepared bread, as she always did. Perhaps she stood a little longer in the doorway, watching her son shoulder his travel sack, knowing something in her soul would never be the same. Yeshua's departure was not marked by trumpets. It was not attended by angels (not visibly). He left as quietly as he had lived. But something had shifted.

He was not going on a journey.

He was stepping into destiny.

The time of building in obscurity was complete. Now, he would build in the open. The workshop of silence was closing. The ministry of light was about to begin.

The River of Prophetic Fulfillment

The Jordan River had always been more than water. It was a threshold.

It was the river the Israelites crossed to enter the Promised Land. It was the river Elijah struck with his mantle before ascending in fire. It was the river where Naaman was healed of leprosy after humbling himself.

Now, it was the place where the Messiah would be revealed.

John the Baptist, Yeshua's cousin and forerunner, was preparing the people—not for religion, but for revolution. He baptized not for ritual but for repentance. He wore camel's hair, ate locusts, and thundered like the prophets of old. He was the voice crying in the wilderness:

> *"Prepare the way of the Lord, make straight paths for him."*
> *—Isaiah 40:3*

He had seen many come through those waters, but none like this one.

The Baptism of Obedience

> *"Then Jesus came from Galilee to the Jordan to be baptized by John."*
> *"But John tried to deter him, saying, 'I need to be baptized by you, and do you come to me?'"*
> *—Matthew 3:13–14*

John knew who stood before him. He had leapt in the womb when Mary entered his mother's house. He had heard the stories. He had felt the Holy Spirit stir.

But Yeshua insisted: "Let it be so now; it is proper for us to do this to fulfill all righteousness." (Matthew 3:15)

Fulfill.

A word that would define his life. Not to break the Law, but to fulfill it.

Not to seek glory, but to submit to the Father.

Not to rush into miracles, but to walk in perfect alignment.

He who had no sin entered the waters of repentance to identify with those who did. He who had nothing to confess stepped into the same river as the broken and the lost.

He who was fully divine submitted to the sign of cleansing to sanctify it for the rest of us.

And in that moment—wet, bowed, surrendered—the heavens opened.

The Voice and the Dove

"As soon as Jesus was baptized, he went up out of the water. At that moment heaven was opened, and he saw the Spirit of God descending like a dove and alighting on him. And a voice from heaven said,

'This is my Son, whom I love; with him I am well pleased."
—Matthew 3:16–17

After thirty years of silence, Heaven spoke.

After thirty years of waiting, the Father affirmed.

"This is my Son."

The identity of Yeshua was not up for debate. It was declared by the only voice that mattered.

"Whom I love."

The foundation of ministry was not performance—but belovedness.

"With Him I am well pleased."

Before a single miracle, before a single sermon, before calling disciples or raising the dead—the Father declared His pleasure.

Yeshua's identity was not achieved. It was received. And every son and daughter of God must begin here.

The Anointing of the Spirit

The Spirit did not descend like fire or thunder. Not like at Sinai. Not like at Pentecost. It came like a dove—gentle, light, clean.

It rested on him.

It did not rush past. It did not hover at a distance.

It remained.

This was the anointing not just for miracles, but for mission.

Not just for power, but for presence.

Not just to heal bodies, but to break yokes.

This was the same Spirit that hovered over the waters in Genesis.

The same Spirit that led prophets, empowered judges, filled kings.

Now it rested on the Carpenter from Nazareth. The Kingdom had begun.

The Cornerstone Is Set At this moment, the cornerstone was fully set— not in stone, but in Spirit.

> *"See, I lay a stone in Zion, a chosen and precious*
> *cornerstone, and the one who trusts in him will never*
> *be put to shame."*
> *—1 Peter 2:6*

Yeshua was that stone.

Rejected by men.

Chosen by God.

Laid not by human hands, but by the divine hand of history.

Everything from this moment forward would be built on him.

His teachings. His miracles.

His disciples. His Church.

His Cross.

His resurrection.

But the cornerstone was laid before all of it—in water, in surrender, in love.

The Builder Becomes the Temple

John the Baptist had pointed and said, "Behold, the Lamb of God."

But what he beheld was not just a lamb—it was the future temple of God, walking in sandals.

Yeshua would soon declare,

> *"Destroy this temple, and I will raise it again in three days."*
> *—John 2:19*

He spoke of his body. The temple had moved.

No longer confined to stone walls in Jerusalem.

No longer behind veils and guarded doors.

The presence of God now walked in the flesh, smiled through eyes, reached with hands, and spoke in parables.

And all of it began—not in a crowd or on a throne—but in the quiet waters of the Jordan.

Conclusion: The Waters that Still Speak

Before the Cross, before the crowds, before the Upper Room,

There was the river. There was obedience. There was a voice.

The cornerstone was set not with fanfare, but with faith.

Not with acclaim, but with alignment.

Not with power, but with peace.

And it calls to us still. Because we, too, are invited:

To enter the waters of surrender.

To rest in the identity of belovedness.

To build not on applause, but on the pleasure of the Father.

Yeshua's early life—his birth, his exile, his craftsmanship, his hiddenness, and his baptism—was not wasted time. It was the blueprint of how Heaven builds.

Quietly. Faithfully. Layer by layer. Stone by stone.

Until the whole house rests secure on the Rock.

The cornerstone is set.

The Kingdom is coming. And the Builder has taken his place.

EPILOGUE

The Builder and the Kingdom

He never wore a crown of gold.

He wore sawdust. Sweat. Later, thorns.

He never carried blueprints rolled under his arm.

He carried beams, burdens, and blessings.

He never laid bricks or raised palaces.

He built something deeper. Something invisible.

Something unshakable.

He built the Kingdom of God.

And he built it not from above, but from among.

From stone floors and dirt roads, From Nazareth's hills and Jordan's waters.

From parables whispered in olive groves and truths declared in synagogues, From compassion, confrontation, cross, and resurrection—He built.

> *A Kingdom Not of This World*
> *"My Kingdom is not of this world..."*
> *—John 18:36*

And yet—he built it in the world.

Among the laborers and lepers, the fishermen and Pharisees.

He didn't gather armies or demand taxes. He gathered hearts.

He didn't construct walls. He broke them down.

He didn't ask for bricks. He asked for belief.

Yeshua's Kingdom was not founded on land or law, but on love.

Not on control, but on conviction.

Not on conquest, but on communion.

And those first building blocks?

A teenage girl who said yes. A builder who obeyed dreams.

A wilderness prophet who pointed.

A few fishermen who left nets behind.

A tax collector who walked away from his wealth.

It wasn't architecture. It was allegiance.

The Living Stones

> *"You also, like living stones, are being built into a spiritual house..."*
> *—1 Peter 2:5*

The Builder is still building. Only now, the raw materials are us.

Each of us, chiseled and shaped, placed precisely where grace has designed:

The broken, mended and made useful.

The overlooked, set in prominent places.

The rejected, made into cornerstones.

We are not just followers— we are construction.

Each act of obedience is a beam.

Each word of truth, a nail. Each prayer, a pillar.

Each forgiveness, a foundation.

Yeshua does not build with machinery.

He builds with mercy.

He does not draft on paper. He drafts on hearts.

And slowly, eternally, he raises something that cannot fall.

The Blueprint: His Life

The blueprint was never hidden. It was lived.

Born in vulnerability.

Sheltered in Egypt.

Raised in labor.

Formed in silence.

Revealed in water.

Empowered by Spirit.

Proven in wilderness.

Embodied in healing.

Anchored in truth.

Sealed in blood.

Crowned in resurrection.

This is how God builds.

Not in haste, but in holiness. Not in ambition, but in alignment.

Not in flashes, but in faithfulness.

And if this was Yeshua's path—It is ours too.

The Kingdom Within You.

> *"The Kingdom of God is within you."*
> *—Luke 17:21*

That Kingdom—the one Yeshua spent thirty years preparing for, and three years revealing—is not far away. It does not sit on a throne in Jerusalem or behind a gate of gold.

It is here. In you.

Being built every day. Stone by stone.

Choice by choice. Love by love.

The same Spirit that descended on him like a dove now dwells in us.

The same Father who said, "This is my Son, in whom I am well pleased" now looks upon us through the righteousness of that Son—and smiles still.

You, reader, are not incidental to this story.

You are the next generation of stones.

Not cold, not dead—living stones.

Called to carry what he carried.

To build what he began. To wait as he waited.

To love as he loved.

The Return of the Builder

One day, he will return—not as a child in straw or a carpenter with calloused hands, but as the King of Glory, riding not a donkey, but the clouds.

And the work he began in Nazareth, through sweat and silence, he will finish with fire and finality.

> *"Behold, I am making all things new."*
> *—Revelation 21:5*

The Builder is not done.

The Kingdom is not finished. The blueprint is still unfolding.

But the cornerstone is set.

Unmoving. Unshaken. Eternal.

A Final Reflection Yeshua the Builder—Whose tools were love and truth, Whose material was hearts and hope, Whose legacy is still rising like a holy temple in every nation—Did not begin in fame. He began in faith.

He began in family. He began in faithful obscurity.

And that is where the greatest things are still being born.

So build. Build in silence. Build with joy.

Build in obedience. Build as he built—Knowing the Kingdom is rising stone by living stone.

And the Builder walks beside you.

It is finished.

But it is only beginning.

The Kingdom of God is at hand.

Scripture References

Chapter One – Born in Bethlehem, Destined for Glory

Micah 5:2 – "But thou, Bethlehem Ephratah... out of thee shall he come forth unto me that is to be ruler in Israel..."

Luke 2:7 – "And she brought forth her firstborn son... and laid him in a manger..."

Luke 2:8–14 – Angel appears to shepherds: "Glory to God in the highest, and on earth peace..."

Luke 2:19 – "But Mary kept all these things, and pondered them in her heart."

Matthew 2:11 – "And when they were come into the house, they saw the young child with Mary his mother..."

Matthew 2:16 – Herod kills the children: "...slew all the children that were in Bethlehem... from two years old and under."

Matthew 7:24–27 – The wise and foolish builders: "...built his house upon a rock..."

John 6:35 – "I am the bread of life: he that cometh to me shall never hunger..."

Chapter Two – The Refugee Messiah: Egypt and Exile

Matthew 2:13–15 – Flight into Egypt: "Arise... flee into Egypt... Out of Egypt have I called my son."

Hosea 11:1 – "When Israel was a child, then I loved him, and called my son out of Egypt."

Matthew 2:18 – "In Rama was there a voice heard, lamentation, and weeping…"

Matthew 2:19–23 – Return from Egypt and settling in Nazareth: "…he shall be called a Nazarene."

Chapter Three – Nazareth: A Builder's School of Obedience

Luke 2:39–40 –"And the child grew, and waxed strong in spirit…"

Luke 2:51–52 – "…and was subject unto them… And Jesus increased in wisdom and stature…"

Mark 6:3 – "Is not this the carpenter, the son of Mary…?"

Chapter Four – Tekton: The Hands That Shaped Stone

Matthew 13:55 – "Is not this the carpenter's son?"

Matthew 6:24 – "No man can serve two masters…"

Luke 14:28 – "For which of you, intending to build a tower, sitteth not down first…"

Matthew 21:42 – "The stone which the builders rejected… is become the head of the corner."

Psalm 118:22 – "The stone which the builders refused is become the head stone of the corner."

1 Peter 2:4–5 – "Ye also, as lively stones, are built up a spiritual house…"

John 14:2 – "In my Father's house are many mansions… I go to prepare a place for you."

Chapter Five – The Boy in the Temple: Twelve and Timeless

Luke 2:41–50 –Journey to Jerusalem, Jesus among the teachers: "… Wist ye not that I must be about my Father's business?"

Luke 2:51–52 –"And he went down with them… and was subject unto them…"

Isaiah 9:6 – "…and the government shall be upon his shoulder…"

Luke 1:46–49 –Mary's Magnificat (used in reflection)

Mark 6:4 – "A prophet is not without honour, but in his own country…"

Chapter Six – The Hidden Years: The Silent Formation

Genesis 2:15 – "And the Lord God took the man, and put him into the garden… to dress it and to keep it."

Hebrews 5:8 – "Though he were a Son, yet learned he obedience by the things which he suffered."

Luke 17:21 – "…for, behold, the kingdom of God is within you."

Chapter Seven – Before the Baptism: The Cornerstone Is Set

Matthew 3:1–17 – Baptism of Jesus: "This is my beloved Son, in whom I am well pleased."

Isaiah 40:3 – "The voice of him that crieth in the wilderness, Prepare ye the way of the Lord…"

John 1:29 – "Behold the Lamb of God, which taketh away the sin of the world."

1 Peter 2:6 – "Behold, I lay in Sion a chief corner stone, elect, precious…"

John 2:19 –"Destroy this temple, and in three days I will raise it up."

Revelation 21:5 – "Behold, I make all things new."

Works Cited and Consulted

Ancient and Jewish Sources

Josephus, Flavius. Antiquities of the Jews. Translated by William Whiston. Hendrickson Publishers, 1987.

Mishnah and Talmud. Selected tractates on Temple customs, early childhood formation, and pilgrimage traditions. Cited for historical - cultural insight.

Biblical Commentaries and Theology

Bailey, Kenneth E. Jesus Through Middle Eastern Eyes: Cultural Studies in the Gospels. IVP Academic, 2008.

Insight on honor-shame culture, village life in Nazareth, and Yeshua's childhood context.

Brown, Raymond E. The Birth of the Messiah: A Commentary on the Infancy Narratives in Matthew and Luke. Doubleday, 1993.

Critical study of the infancy accounts with historical reconstruction and theological commentary.

Keener, Craig S. The IVP Bible Background Commentary: New Testament. InterVarsity Press, 1993.

Background on Greco- Roman culture, Jewish customs, and scriptural context.

Wright, N.T. Jesus and the Victory of God. Fortress Press, 1996.

Theological analysis of Jesus' mission, identity, and first-century expectations of the Messiah.

France, R.T. The Gospel of Matthew. New International Commentary on the New Testament. Eerdmans, 2007.

Extensive exegetical detail on Matthew 1–3 and related prophecy fulfillment.

Historical and Archaeological Resources

Burge, Gary M., and Gene A. Green. The New Testament in Antiquity: A Survey of the New Testament Within Its Cultural Contexts. Zondervan Academic, 2009.

For understanding Nazareth, Sepphoris, and building trades in first-century Galilee.

Safrai, Shmuel. The Jewish People in the First Century. Vol. 1. Compiled by the Historical Society of Israel.

Social and religious structure in Yeshua's early environment.

Jeremias, Joachim. Jerusalem in the Time of Jesus. Fortress Press, 1969.

Deep dive into socioeconomic and religious life in first-century Palestine.

Scripture Versions

The Holy Bible, King James Version (KJV). Public domain
translation used throughout this work.

Acknowledgments

To write of Yeshua's early life is to walk on holy ground. Every word in this book was carved not merely from study, but from reverence, prayer, and awe. And no work of this magnitude is ever done alone.

First and foremost, I thank Feebe Huang, my beloved wife—your faith, your wisdom, and your unwavering belief in God's timing have carried me through every page of this journey. You are the quiet strength behind each sentence, the echo of heaven in my daily life, and my most cherished companion in this calling.

To those who raised me, taught me, prayed over me, and believed in the fire God placed in my bones—you are part of this architecture.

To the rabbis, scholars, and pastors—both ancient and modern— whose insight and sacrifice helped illuminate the dusty roads of Nazareth, Egypt, and Galilee—I walk in your shadow with humility.

To every soul reading this now—whether you hold a hammer, a pen, a prayer, or a broken past—know this: you are part of the house God is building.

And to the Builder Himself.

—Yeshua, the Nazarene, the Refugee, the Redeemer—this book is my offering at your feet. May it stir hearts, awaken wonder, and bring many back to the cornerstone.

About the Author

Damiano B. Centola is a theologian, poet, and author whose works blend biblical scholarship with spiritual passion. His writings explore the mystery, beauty, and truth of Scripture, bringing ancient truths into living clarity for today's world. With a background in theology, culture, and prophetic insight, Damiano has authored multiple books including God's

Sovereignty: Exploring the Divine Rule Over Creation, History, and Eternity, Divine Encounters: Discovering the Depth and Power of God's Names, and The Mother of Corruption: Unveiling Spiritual Corruption from Babylon to Today.

He writes with a rare fusion of reverence, poetic fire, and scholarly depth, inviting readers to rediscover the majesty of God's design and the call to walk in truth.

Damiano lives with his wife, Feebe, and continues his mission to awaken hearts, elevate minds, and build bridges between the sacred and the everyday.

Other Books by Damiano B. Centola

God's Sovereignty: Exploring the Divine Rule Over Creation, History, and Eternity

A profound journey through Scripture, history, and the nature of divine control—guiding readers to trust God's hand in every season.

The Mother of Corruption: Unveiling Spiritual Corruption from Babylon to Today

A bold exposé tracing the spiritual deception that has shaped empires, institutions, and modern culture—through prophecy, history, and truth.

Divine Encounters: Discovering the Depth and Power of God's Names

A rich devotional exploring the sacred names of God across Scripture, revealing His character, power, and intimate presence.

I Choose the Call: My Daily Anthem of Devotion

A Journey of Faith, Purpose, and Obedience A 365-day devotional calling readers into deeper intimacy with God, purpose- driven living, and unwavering obedience.

The Lord Is My Shepherd: A Journey

Through Psalm 23—Meditations on Trust, Hope, and Eternal Love

A pastoral meditation on the most beloved psalm, unpacking its eternal promises for the weary, the hopeful, and the devoted.

Jewish Holidays: Jesus Teaches Us Through Sacred Seasons

A scholarly and spiritual guide to the biblical feasts— revealing how each sacred season points to Yeshua the Messiah.

The Words of Jesus: Unlocking the Lord's Prayer in Aramaic, Greek, and English

A tri-lingual unveiling of the Lord's Prayer, illuminating its original meaning and restoring its power through the languages Yeshua spoke and understood.

Note on Proportions and Diagrams

The proportions and diagrams presented in this book are intended to illustrate symbolic, theological, and historical insights drawn from Scripture, art, and sacred geometry. While grounded in anatomical and mathematical research, they represent interpretive models rather than clinical or universally precise measurements of the human body. Their purpose is not to claim absolute scientific accuracy but to reveal the patterns by which artists, architects, and theologians have discerned divine order in creation.

www.ingramcontent.com/pod-product-compliance
Lightning Source LLC
Chambersburg PA
CBHW051235120626
46547CB00013B/1653